CONDUCTOR

T0041096

PLAY ALONG WITH THE CANADIAN BRASS

15 INTERMEDIATE PIECES

Trumpets: Ryan Anthony,
Joe Burgstaller
Horn: Jeff Nelsen
Trombone: Gene Watts
Tuba: Chuck Daellenbach

To access companion recorded performances online, visit:
www.halleonard.com/mylibrary

Enter Code
2075-1086-7344-9247

Recorded 2001, Toronto; Rob Tremills, engineer

7777 W. BLUEMOUND RD. P.O. BOX 13819 MILWAUKEE, WI 53213

Visit Hal Leonard Online at
www.halleonard.com
Visit Canadian Brass online at
www.canbrass.com

PLAY ALONG WITH THE CANADIAN BRASS

15 INTERMEDIATE PIECES

THE CANADIAN BRASS

Contents

The price of this publication includes access to companion recorded performances online, for download or streaming, using the unique code found on the title page.

ANDANTE
from the Trumpet Concerto

Joseph Haydn
(1732-1809)
arranged by Walter Barnes

PRAYER
from *Hansel and Gretel*

Engelbert Humperdinck
(1854-1921)
arranged by Henry Charles Smith

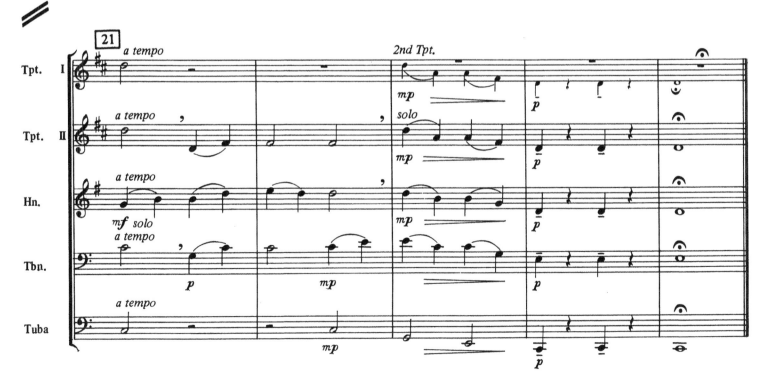

RONDEAU

Jean-Joseph Mouret
(1682-1738)
arranged by Walter Barnes

PILGRIMS' CHORUS

from *Tannhäuser*

Richard Wagner
(1813-1883)
arranged by Henry Charles Smith

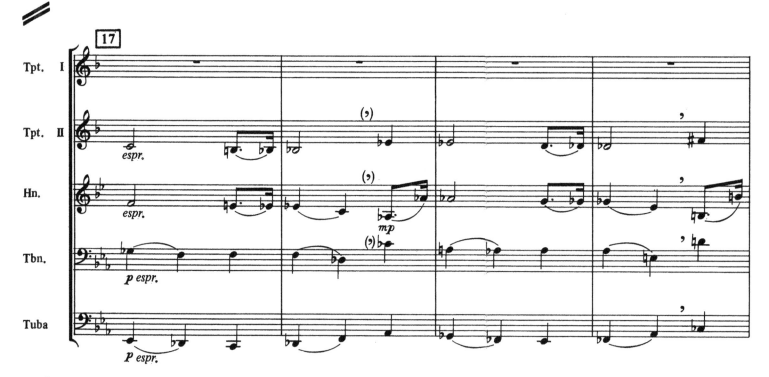

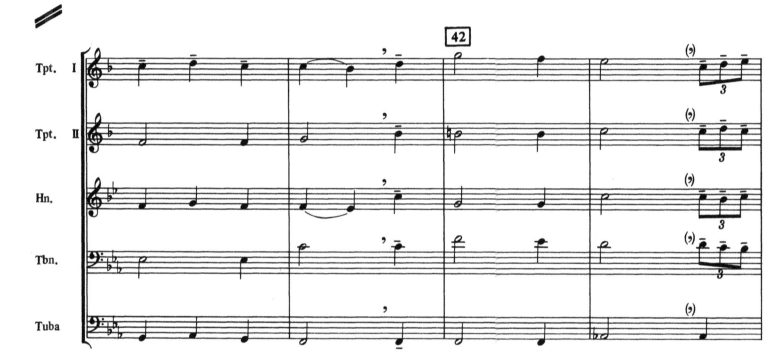

CANON

Johann Pachelbel
(1653-1706)
arranged by Walter Barnes

WHERE'ER YOU WALK

from *Semele*

George Frideric Handel
(1685-1759)
arranged by Walter Barnes

In a singing manner; ♩=96

1st Tpt.

2nd Tpt.

Hn. in F

Tbn.

Tuba

29 Where'er You Walk *continued*

39

45

GRAND MARCH
from *Aïda*

Giuseppi Verdi
(1813-1901)
arranged by Walter Barnes

23 Grand March from Aida *continued*

45 Grand March from Aida *continued*

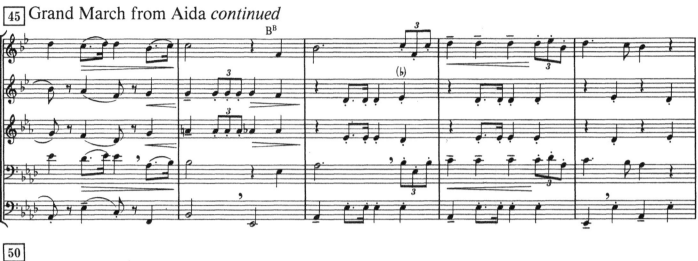

50

55

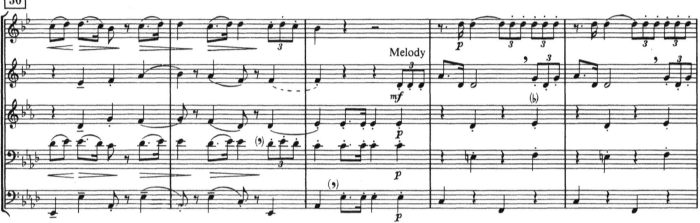

60

65 Grand March from Aida *continued*

69

THREE ELIZABETHAN MADRIGALS

I. My Bonny Lass, She Smileth

Thomas Morely
(1557-1602)
arranged by Walter Barnes

40 Three Elizabethan Madrigals *continued*

II. Come Again, Sweet Love

John Dowland
(1562-1626)
arranged by Walter Barnes

III. Now is the Month of Maying

Thomas Morely
(1557-1602)
arranged by Walter Barnes

TRUMPET VOLUNTARY

John Stanley
(1713-1786)
arranged by Walter Barnes

34 Trumpet Voluntary *continued*

THREE SPIRITUALS

African-American spirituals
arranged by Walter Barnes

Three Spirituals *continued*

75 Three Spirituals *continued*

103 Three Spirituals *continued*

111

AMADING GRACE

traditional American
arranged by Luther Henderson
adapted by Walter Barnes

40